Let's Trade

A Book About Bartering

by Nancy Loewen　*　illustrated by Brian Jensen

Thanks to our advisers for their expertise, research, and advice:

Dr. Joseph Santos
Associate Professor of Economics, Department of Economics
South Dakota State University

Susan Kesselring, M.A., Literacy Educator
Rosemount–Apple Valley–Eagan (Minnesota) School District

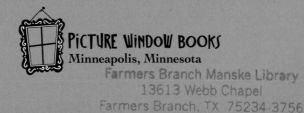

PICTURE WINDOW BOOKS
Minneapolis, Minnesota

Social Studies

Editorial Director: Carol Jones
Managing Editor: Catherine Neitge
Creative Director: Keith Griffin
Editor: Christianne Jones
Story Consultant: Terry Flaherty
Designer: Joe Anderson
Page Production: Picture Window Books
The illustrations in this book were created digitally.

Picture Window Books
5115 Excelsior Boulevard
Suite 232
Minneapolis, MN 55416
877-845-8392
www.picturewindowbooks.com

Printed in the United States of America.

Library of Congress Cataloging-in-Publication Data
Loewen, Nancy, 1964-
Let's trade : a book about bartering / by Nancy Loewen ;
illustrated by Brian Jensen.
p. cm. — (Money matters)
Includes bibliographical references and index.
ISBN 1-4048-1157-5 (hardcover)
1. Barter—Juvenile literature. 2. Exchange—Juvenile
literature. I. Jensen, Brian, ill. II. Title. III. Money matters
(Minneapolis, Minn.)

HF1019.L642 2006
332'.54—dc22   2005004064

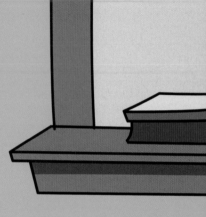

It was social studies time, and Mr. Wallace was supposed to be talking about money. Instead, he said, "I skipped breakfast, and I'm starving! Does anyone have a snack?"

"You could have these crackers," Ryan said.

"I couldn't just take them," Mr. Wallace said. "Class, what could I do to get those crackers and still be fair to Ryan?"

"You could pay for them," Angela said.

"But I left my wallet at home," Mr. Wallace said. "Without money, is there any way I can get those crackers?"

"Maybe you could trade something for them," Tyrone said.

People usually depend on money to get the things they need. But sometimes there are other ways.

5

"Great idea! I could find something that's about the same value as the crackers, and we could trade. But what if I don't have anything to trade?" Mr. Wallace asked.

"You could do something for Ryan, like clean his desk," Nicki said.

Goods are items that are made and sold. Services are acts that people can do to help others.

6

"Excellent!" Mr. Wallace said. "Class, you've just learned the basics of bartering. To barter means to trade. It can be trading goods, or it can be trading services. You barter all the time. Can someone give me an example?"

"When we switch sandwiches at lunch," said Melissa.

"Trading sports cards," offered Steven.

"When our parents take turns taking us to soccer games," José said.

Trading goods and services is a part of everyday life.

9

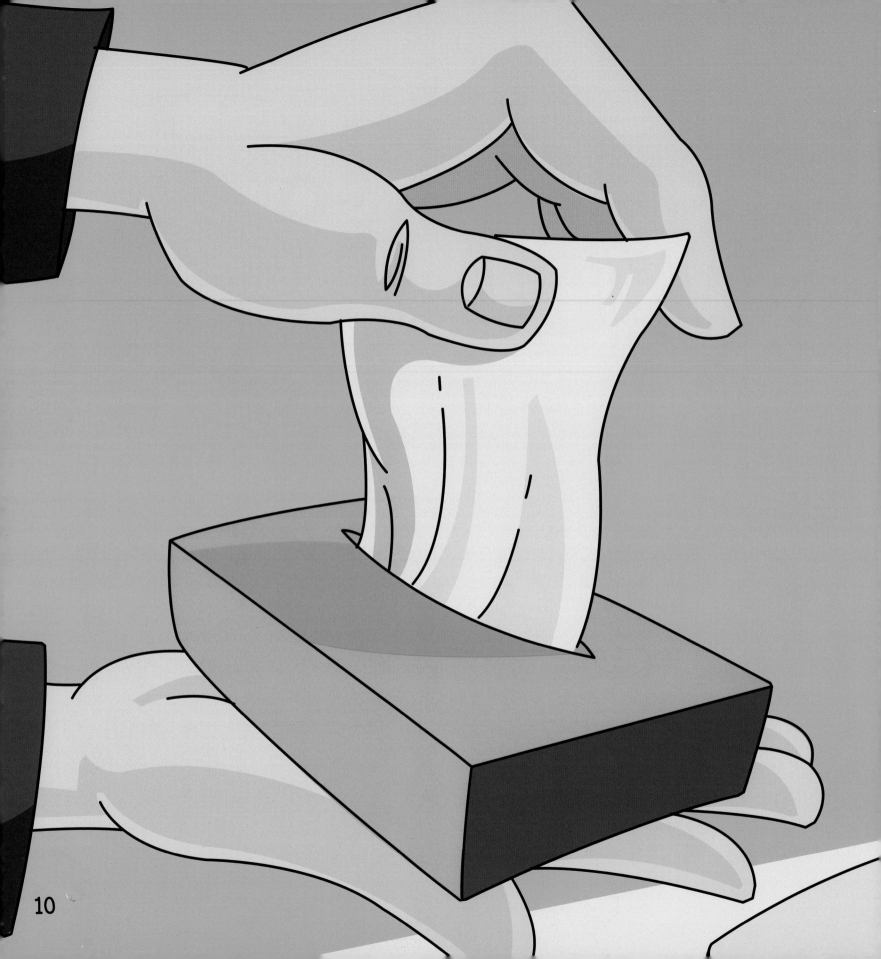

"Good examples!" Mr. Wallace said. "Let's think about bartering a little more. Ryan, what if I'd offered you a box of tissues for your crackers? Would you have traded?"

"No way! I don't really need the tissues. I'd rather keep the crackers," Ryan said.

In the fairy tale "Jack and the Beanstalk," Jack trades his cow for a few beans. His mother is very angry about the poor trade until she realizes the beans are magic.

"Right," said Mr. Wallace. "For bartering to work well, two things need to happen. Both people have to want or need the things being traded, and the things being traded have to be worth about the same value."

"A long time ago," Mr. Wallace said, "people didn't have money. They had to trade for the things they needed. Someone might trade a basket of wheat for an ax, and that was fine as long as both people wanted those things. But what if the person with the ax already had plenty of wheat? The person with the wheat might trade for something else first—a pearl necklace, maybe. Then, he would trade the necklace for the ax."

14

Mr. Wallace continued.
"That kind of indirect
trading was the beginning
of our money system.
People traded based on
ideas, rather than things."

The first forms of money
were animals and grain.

"All that trading sounds like an awful lot of work!" Claire exclaimed.

"It was," said Mr. Wallace. "Gradually, people started using money, but bartering has always been around."

16

He continued. "During the 1930s, the United States went through the Great Depression. Banks closed, businesses lost money, and millions of people were suddenly broke and out of work. People bartered whenever they could. Bartering is sometimes used today."

When people are unsure of what the nation's currency (money) is worth, they are more likely to barter.

"Now, we're going to play a game," Mr. Wallace said.

He divided the class into three groups. He gave the first group a box of unsharpened pencils. He gave the second group a box of pencil-top erasers. He gave the third group a pencil sharpener.

"The goal of this game," Mr. Wallace said, "is for every group to end up with sharpened pencils with erasers on top. Go!"

Everyone started trading. Pencils for erasers—erasers for sharpening—sharpening for pencils. The classroom became very noisy!

"We did it!" the students exclaimed when all the groups had sharpened pencils with erasers on top.

"Nice work!" said Mr. Wallace. "I can see you're all naturals when it comes to bartering. There's just one problem. I'm STILL hungry. Ryan, would you trade your crackers for my lucky pen?"

"You've got yourself a deal!" said Ryan.

A Day of Trading

>> You and your friend have a fun Saturday afternoon planned, but your bike has a flat tire. You need to borrow your brother's bike, but he's using it. He says he will lend you his bike if you clean his room. You really need his bike, so you clean his room. Did you make a fair trade?

>> You meet your friend at the park. You both brought activities. You brought a comic book to read, and your friend brought his flying disc. Your friend really wants the comic book for his collection. You trade your comic book for the flying disc. Did you make a fair trade?

>> Next, you and your friend go to Collector's Corner, which is your favorite store. You both buy a pack of baseball cards. Your friend got your favorite player's card. You trade him three of your cards for one of his. Did you make a fair trade?

>> Then, the two of you go to the arcade. You only have dollar bills, and the change machine is broken. You really want to play the racing game. Your friend has some change, but it's only three quarters. You give him one dollar bill for the three quarters so you can play the game. Did you make a fair trade?

>> Finally, it's time for some treats. You can't decide what you want. You order onion rings, and your friend orders french fries. You give him five onion rings, and he gives you ten fries. Did you make a fair trade?

It's time to go home. What a day of trading!

Fun Facts

- The first money made of metal was developed in China around 1000 B.C.

- The early colonists often traded deerskin. A male deer is called a buck. The word came to mean dollar, too. The colonists also traded items such as beaver pelts, nails, and corn.

- About $16 billion worth of products and services are still bartered in the United States today.

- Businesses often barter with each other to exchange their unused inventory, or products. Governments barter as well.

Glossary

colonists—people living in a colony or a land that is newly settled

goods—things that are sold

Great Depression—a period in the United States in the 1930s when many businesses failed and people lost jobs

natural resources—things in nature that people use, such as coal and trees

services—useful work

value—how much something is worth

To LEARN MoRE

At the Library

Godfrey, Neale. *Neale S. Godfrey's Ultimate Kids Money Book*. New York: Simon and Schuster, 1998.

Hall, Kirsten. *Let's Trade:All About Trading*. New York: Children's Press, 2004.

Maestro, Betsy. *The Story of Money*. New York: Mulberry Books, 1995.

On the Web

FactHound offers a safe, fun way to find Web sites related to this book. All of the sites on FactHound have been researched by our staff. *www.facthound.com*

1. Visit the FactHound home page.

2. Enter a search word related to this book, or type in this special code: 1404811575

3. Click on the FETCH IT button.

Your trusty FactHound will fetch the best sites for you!

Look for all of the books in the Money Matters series:

- Cash, Credit Cards, or Checks: A Book About Payment Methods
- In the Money: A Book About Banking
- Lemons and Lemonade: A Book About Supply and Demand
- Let's Trade: A Book About Bartering
- Save, Spend, or Donate? A Book About Managing Money
- Taxes, Taxes! Where the Money Goes
- Ups and Downs: A Book About the Stock Market
- That Costs Two Shells: The History of Money